MEET THE GREATS

Martin Luther KING Jr.

TIM COOKE

Gareth Stevens PUBLISHING

Please visit our website, **www.garethstevens.com**.
For a free color catalog of all our high-quality books,
call toll free 1-800-542-2595 or fax 1-877-542-2596.

CATALOGING-IN-PUBLICATION DATA

Names: Cooke, Tim.
Title: Martin Luther King Jr. / Tim Cooke.
Description: New York : Gareth Stevens, 2017. | Series: Meet the greats | Includes index.
Identifiers: ISBN 9781482459524 (pbk.) | ISBN 9781482459548 (library bound) | ISBN 9781482459531 (6 pack)
Subjects: LCSH: King, Martin Luther, Jr., 1929-1968--Juvenile literature. | African Americans--Civil rights--History--20th century--Juvenile literature. | Civil rights workers--United States--Biography--Juvenile literature.
Classification: LCC E185.97.K5 C66 2017 | DDC 323.092--dc23

Published in 2017 by
Gareth Stevens Publishing
111 East 14th Street, Suite 349
New York, NY 10003

For Brown Bear Books Ltd:
Editorial Director: Lindsey Lowe
Managing Editor: Tim Cooke
Children's Publisher: Anne O'Daly
Design Manager: Keith Davis
Designer and illustrator: Supriya Sahai
Picture Manager: Sophie Mortimer

Concept development: Square and Circus / Brown Bear Books Ltd

Picture Credits: Front Cover: Character artwork, Supriya Sahai. Interior: All photographs Library of Congress except, Robert Hunt Library: 18, 21, 29, 34, 35, 38; Shutterstock: 25b Steven Frame 43, mark Van Scyoc 40; US National Archives: 36; Wikipedia: Cornell University/Kheel Center 41, Federal Bureau of Prisons 42t, Fowler & Fowler 20, Lyndon Baines Johnson Library and Museum/Yochi Okamoto 39, National Civil Rights Museum/Adam Jones, PH.D, 22t, WHPO/Cecil Stoughton 39.

All rights reserved. No part of this book may be reproduced in any form without permission from the publisher, except by a reviewer.

Printed in China
CPSIA compliance information: Batch CW17GS: For further information contact Gareth Stevens, New York, New York at 1-800-542-2595.

Contents

Introduction 4
Called to the Church 6
Feature: The Civil Rights Movement 14
Trouble in Birmingham 16
Feature: Under Investigation 24
Civil Rights Leader 26
Feature: "I Have a Dream" 34
The Assassination 36
Timeline 44
Glossary 46
Further Resources 47
Index 48

Introduction

Martin Luther King Jr. was born into a world where he did not enjoy the same rights or opportunities as white Americans.

At the start of the 1960s, a hundred years after America fought a civil war (1861–1865) over the question of whether or not to allow slavery, African Americans were still being treated badly by white Americans. In the South, they did not have the same rights as their white neighbors. African Americans were not allowed to use the same schools, bathrooms, pools, hotels or restaurants as white Americans. They also had separate entrances to facilities and separate water fountains, and they had to sit in back of public buses.

Many people wanted to change this. One man, Martin Luther King Jr., became a leader of the **civil rights** movement. He wanted African Americans to be treated the same as white Americans. He dedicated his short life to fighting for African Americans to achieve civil rights through peaceful means. He was awarded the Nobel Prize for Peace in 1964. Four years later he was shot dead.

"I have a dream ..."

Called to the CHURCH

Martin Luther King Jr. was a devoted Christian. He was working as a pastor when he emerged as a civil rights leader.

Martin Luther King Jr. was born on January 15, 1929, in Atlanta, Georgia. His grandparents had been slaves but Martin's parents were financially comfortable. His father Martin was the pastor at the Ebenezer Baptist Church in Atlanta. Martin was the middle of three children. He had an older sister and a younger brother. The children lived with their parents, grandparents, uncles and aunts in a large house in Atlanta.

Martin's home in Atlanta.

QUICK FACTS

- Martin was born when the South was still segregated.
- He became a pastor in the Baptist church–just like his own father!

This cinema has a separate entrance for black patrons.

RACIST SOCIETY

Atlanta lay in the South, where **discrimination** against African Americans was common. Local and state laws known as **Jim Crow laws** treated blacks as second-class citizens. Black schools, for example, did not have as many funds as white schools. Martin's father taught his children that all people were equal in God's eyes. One day when Martin was small, he was riding with his father in his car. A white policeman stopped them. The policeman called Martin's father "boy." White people often called African American men "boy" to show a lack of respect. Martin's father pointed at his son and said, "That is a boy. I am a man." Martin Jr. never forgot his father's bravery.

A SMART KID

Martin studied hard and did well in school. He was small for his size but he was strong and could wrestle much bigger boys to the ground. From a very early age, Martin became aware of the **racist** society he lived in. When he was six years old, his best friend was a white boy. Because of their color, the friends went to different schools. Eventually his friend's father forbade their friendship because of the color of Martin's skin.

When he was 15, Martin won first prize in a public-speaking competition with a speech on "the Negro and the Constitution." He was a powerful **orator**. On the bus home, Martin had to give his seat to a white man under a law called "whites before blacks." Later Martin said, "That night I was the angriest I've ever been in my life."

Even water fountains were segregated in the South.

In summer 1944, Martin visited the North. He worked on a farm in Connecticut. It was the first time he had been treated the same as white people. He could shop in the same stores and eat in the same restaurants. At the end of the summer, he had to return to the **segregated** South.

Morehouse College, Atlanta.

BECOMING A MINISTER

Martin was not sure what career to follow. He thought he might become a lawyer or a doctor. But his principal at Morehouse College in Atlanta suggested that he follow in his father's footsteps and become a minister. The principal thought that would give Martin the best way to work for the social changes he wanted. In 1948, aged just 19 years, Martin was **ordained** as a Baptist minister.

Martin (right) married Coretta in June 1953.

Martin continued his studies in Pennsylvania and Massachusetts. He was awarded a postgraduate doctoral degree in June 1955. By then, he also had a young family. He had married a music student named Coretta Scott in June 1953, and their daughter Yolanda was born in 1955.

STARTING WORK

In 1954, Martin had started work as a preacher in Montgomery, Alabama. He worked hard to attract more people to his church. He gave **sermons** that mixed religious inspiration with practical ideas about how to improve life for African Americans. Martin also became involved with politics. He became the leader of the local branch of the National Association for the Advancement of Colored People (NAACP).

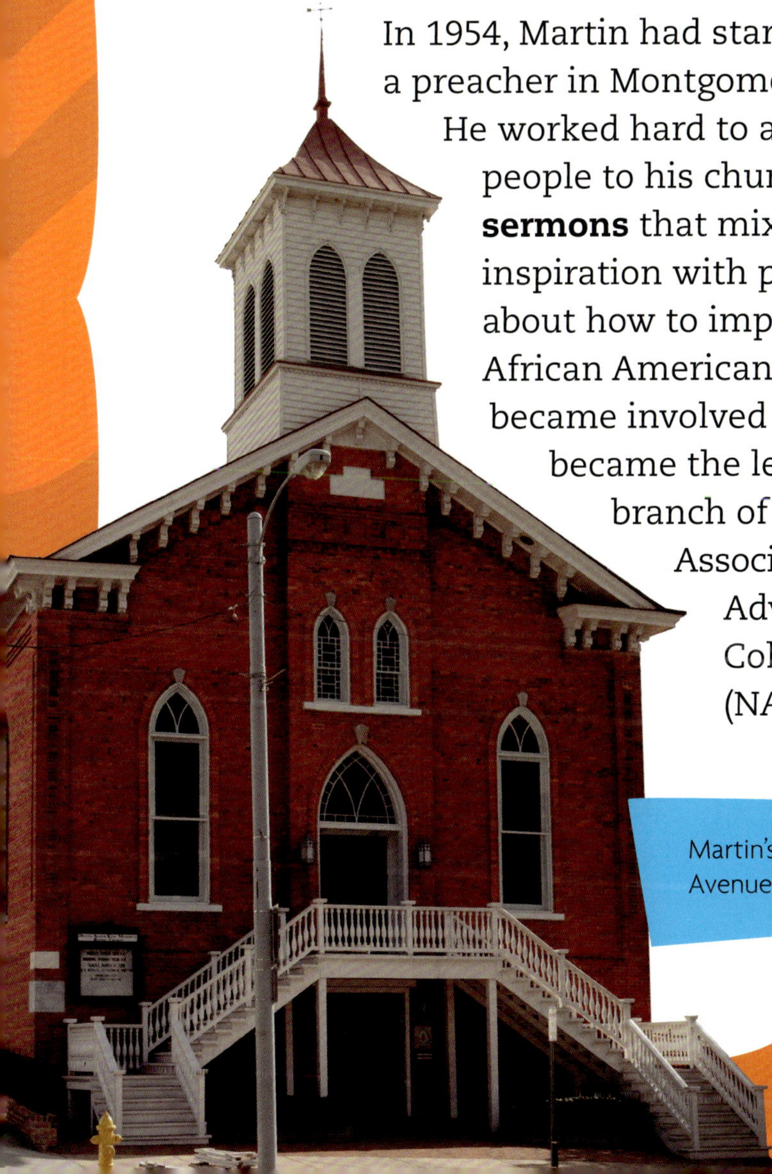

Martin's church on Dexter Avenue in Montgomery.

Rosa Parks has her fingerprints taken by the police.

MONTGOMERY BUS BOYCOTT

On December 1, 1955, African American Rosa Parks refused to give up her bus seat to a white passenger. This broke a Montgomery law that said black bus passengers could not sit in seats reserved for white people. Rosa Parks was arrested. Martin met with other African American leaders. They decided to support her.

Martin and the other leaders urged all African Americans in Montgomery to **boycott** public buses. African Americans took the bus far more than white Americans, so the bus companies soon started losing money. Every week, Martin spoke to African Americans and urged them to carry on their protest. The authorities tried to stop him. Martin was arrested, fined, and even put in jail. His home was firebombed on January 30, 1956, but no one was injured. Still the boycott continued.

After almost a year of the boycott, the protestors won. In November 1956 the U.S. Supreme Court ruled that segregation on public buses was illegal. The next month, Martin and his friends rode the bus. There was no reserved seating for whites. Martin and other African Americans could sit wherever they wanted.

Martin was a powerful preacher and public speaker.

The Civil Rights MOVEMENT

Martin Luther King Jr. was just part of a long struggle to get civil rights for African Americans that matched those of white Americans.

The modern civil rights movement lasted from 1954 to 1968. In fact people had been campaigning for civil rights since 1863, when President Abraham Lincoln freed the slaves in the South. Lincoln said that African Americans had the same rights as white Americans, but in the South those rights were removed by Jim Crow laws. In 1954, the U.S. Supreme Court upheld a doctrine called "separate but equal." It ruled that states and towns could treat black and white Americans differently—as long as they both had equal facilities.

This modern mural portrays civil rights leaders, including Malcolm X (center).

African American protestors at the White House in 1965 demand the right to vote.

A new generation of African leaders believed that facilities for African Americans were not "equal" at all. They argued that it was **unconstitutional** for black and white schools to be segregated. In 1957, the U.S. Supreme Court agreed. Black students could now legally enroll in previously white schools in the South.

One key aim of the civil rights campaign was to get African Americans to register to vote. The more African Americans used their vote to change their politicians, Martin argued, the more they would change their lives. In 1965, Congress passed the Voting Rights Act. It removed many restrictions, and increased the number of African Americans in the South who could vote.

Trouble in BIRMINGHAM

After the desegregation of the Montgomery transportation system, Martin became a leading civil rights figure.

The success of the Montgomery Bus Boycott made Martin well known. His frequent appearances on the national news giving speeches or being interviewed made him a hero to many African Americans. In 1957, Martin stopped working as a church minister in order to campaign for civil rights. He started to travel around America, speaking at public meetings. He also wrote books to spread his ideas. One of his key beliefs was that all protest should be nonviolent. That idea was based on the philosophy of the Indian leader, Mahatma Gandhi.

QUICK FACTS

- Martin insisted that civil rights protests should be peaceful.
- Even so, he was arrested 30 times in his career for protesting in public!

Martin's training as a pastor made him a powerful spokesman for civil rights.

A NEW ORGANIZATION

The success of the bus boycott in Montgomery inspired African Americans in other towns and cities in the South to begin their own campaigns for change. The Southern Christian Leadership Conference (SCLC) was created to organize the campaigns. It was made up of black religious leaders from cities around the South. Martin was its first president.

Martin and the SCLC had two clear aims: to end segregation and to get African Americans to vote.

In 1950s America, local laws sometimes required people to pay a special tax or prove they could read and write in order to vote. But many African Americans were poor or were so badly educated they could not read or write. That meant that out of a possible five million African Americans in the South, only 1.5 million were registered to vote.

Malcolm X disagreed with some of Martin's ideas.

In 1958, Martin began what he called a Crusade for Citizenship. He aimed to double the number of African Americans who could vote in the next election. Martin's campaigns were also making him more famous. That gained him both supporters and enemies. One of his most vocal critics was another African American and civil rights leader, Malcolm X. He did not agree with Martin's policy of nonviolence. He argued that African Americans needed to use violence to make change happen.

The shrine marking the spot where Mahatma Gandhi was killed in 1948.

A NEAR FATAL ATTACK

In September 1958, Martin was in a New York City bookstore signing copies of *Stride Toward Freedom*, his book about the Montgomery protest. A mentally ill African American woman stabbed him in the chest and almost killed him. Martin spent months recovering. During this time, he and Coretta traveled to India. There they visited the **shrine** dedicated to Mahatma Gandhi.

PEACEFUL DEMONSTRATIONS

In 1960, the King family moved back to Atlanta, where the SCLC was based. Martin joined his father's church and again worked as a pastor. He was still involved in the civil rights movement, however. Martin supported four students in Greensboro, North Carolina, who staged a **sit-in** at a segregated lunch counter in February 1960. They refused to move unless they were served.

The students' refusal to be moved inspired a series of nonviolent sit-ins across the South. Martin supported them all. He was arrested during one of them and was sentenced to four months in jail. Martin would be arrested more than 100 times during his lifetime. The next year, 1961, black and white students began to ride on interstate buses, which were still segregated. These Freedom Riders, as they were known, wanted to end segregation on all public transportation in the South.

Four students stage a sit-in at a lunch counter.

Martin's cell in Birmingham Jail.

TROUBLE IN ALABAMA

Martin called Birmingham, Alabama, "the most segregated city in the South." Its police chief, Eugene "Bull" Connor, hated African Americans. His racist views were well known, but the state governor, George Wallace, supported him.

In 1963, Martin began a series of marches and sit-ins in Birmingham to protest segregation. He was arrested and thrown in jail. There he wrote his "Letter from Birmingham Jail" on April 16, 1963. Some Jewish and Christian ministers had suggested that African Americans wait patiently for justice. Martin explained why it was essential to protest. He was not allowed any paper, so he wrote his letter on scraps of newspaper, toilet paper, anything he could find. He was released three days later.

Marchers remember victims killed by a bomb in a Birmingham church.

The world's attention was fixed on Birmingham. On May 2, 1963, a thousand school students marched there to protest segregation. Chief Connor had most of them arrested. The next day, 2,500 more children marched. Connor ordered the police to use water hoses and dogs to break them up. TV cameras sent pictures around the world. On May 5, a group of churchmen marched. This time, the police refused to obey Connor's order to hose the men.

THE PRESIDENT ACTS

The world watched with horror as the police attacked American citizens. President John F. Kennedy realized something had to be done. Unrest was spreading across the South, with protests in more than a hundred cities. In September 1963, white racists bombed an African American church in Birmingham, killing four young girls. Violence was spreading and the jails were full. Kennedy sent the U.S. Army to stop the violence. He also told Congress it was time for a civil rights bill.

President John F. Kennedy.

Under INVESTIGATION

Martin Luther King Jr. was often in trouble with the law. His protests made him unpopular with law enforcement agencies.

Martin was arrested 30 times during his campaign for equal rights for African Americans. As well as being constantly watched by the local and state police, Martin also came to the attention of the Federal Bureau of Investigation (FBI), which dealt with serious crimes. The FBI first noticed Martin as early as December 1955. It began to **monitor** his activities when he got involved in the Montgomery Bus Boycott.

J. Edgar Hoover (1895–1972) was the FBI's director from 1924. Hoover did not like Martin. At the time, many Americans feared that Communists would try to take over America.

J. Edgar Hoover thought Martin was a danger to U.S. security.

Martin meets Robert Kennedy (center).

Hoover believed that Communists were behind the civil rights movement. He ordered **wiretaps** in Martin's home and at the offices of the SCLC, so that he knew who they were talking to. Hoover worried that Martin's influence would lead to African Americans uniting against white Americans, leading to **revolution**.

Martin's phone was bugged so the FBI could tape his calls.

Martin complained about the FBI's treatment of the civil rights movement to Hoover's boss, Attorney General Robert Kennedy. The FBI continued to monitor King until his murder, however. After Martin's death, the Bureau launched an investigation to catch his murderer.

Civil Rights LEADER

Martin and his supporters were gaining in strength. They wanted to force the government to change the civil rights laws.

The world's attention was focused on the Southern states of the United States. The images of Police Chief Eugene "Bull" Connor turning the water hoses on peaceful civil rights protestors in Birmingham, Alabama, had been shown across the world. People were shocked by what they saw. Martin and the other civil rights leaders felt their nonviolent campaign was beginning to have some success. Martin planned to step up the pressure on the U.S. government in his mission to gain civil rights for black Americans.

QUICK FACTS

- Martin and other civil rights leaders organized the March on Washington in August 1963.
- More than 250,000 people turned up!

THE MARCH ON WASHINGTON

Martin and other African American campaigners organized the March for Jobs and Freedom to persuade Congress to pass President Kennedy's Civil Rights Bill. The event is better known as the March on Washington. On August 28, 1963, a quarter of a million protestors gathered in Washington, D.C., to march along the National Mall to the Lincoln Memorial. It was the largest demonstration in American history. The protestors that day included young and old, African Americans and white Americans. Musicians performed, including Bob Dylan, and lots of different speakers addressed the crowd about the need for America to change.

Martin (center of row) walks in the March on Washington.

Martin gives his speech "I Have a Dream."

Martin was the last speaker, and gave his famous "I Have a Dream" speech. The inspirational words confirmed Martin as the main leader of the civil rights movement. Afterward, he met with President Kennedy and Vice President Lyndon B. Johnson to discuss the civil rights bill.

Later that year, on November 22, 1963, President Kennedy was shot dead in Dallas, Texas. Martin was saddened at the murder of someone who had done so much for civil rights. Martin believed that the murder was part of what he called a growing "climate of hate." He told his wife that he feared for his own life. He worried that he would not live to see 40. He would be proved right.

President Johnson signs the Civil Rights Act into law.

WORLD RECOGNITION

In its 1964 New Year edition, *Time* magazine named Martin its "man of the year." His face was on the front cover. In June 1964, Congress passed the Civil Rights Act in honor of the late President Kennedy. The new law meant that segregation was now illegal. In practice, however, African Americans still faced **prejudice** in the South, particularly when it came to voting. African Americans still made up only a small number of voters. In December that year, aged 35, Martin was awarded the Nobel Prize for Peace for his achievements.

Martin was the youngest person ever to win the Nobel Peace Prize. He traveled to Oslo in Norway to accept his award. He gave a moving speech at the ceremony. He described the hate and distrust he said now existed in America between racial groups. He also said that all his $54,000 prize money would go to the fight for civil rights.

At home, Martin continued with his policy of nonviolence. He was increasingly convinced that his most urgent challenge was to get African Americans to register to vote so they could make change happen. In many Southern cities, African Americans made up a small number of voters. In Selma, Alabama, for example, just 350 of the city's 15,000 African Americans were registered to vote. The town's police chief and some of his deputies were known to be racists. Martin decided Selma was where he would concentrate his efforts on persuading African Americans to register to vote.

Protestors show support for the marches in Selma.

In January 1965, Martin joined a demonstration in Selma and was arrested. On March 7, a group of campaigners set out from Selma to walk to the state capital, Montgomery, to **lobby** the racist state governor, George Wallace. The police attacked the peaceful marchers, beating them with whips and clubs wrapped in barbed wire. About 140 marchers were seriously injured. On March 17, after a legal ruling that the march could go ahead, Martin led the protestors again from Selma to Montgomery. President Johnson, in response to the widespread horror at police behavior, rushed the Voting Rights Bill through Congress. It became law in August 1965, marking another victory for civil rights.

DISCONTENT CONTINUES

The summers of 1964 and 1965 saw rioting in black neighborhoods in some cities as African Americans expressed their **frustration** at the lack of equality or economic opportunity. Malcolm X, who led a group called the Nation of Islam, believed that change could only happen through violence. He encouraged the riots. Martin had met Malcolm X only once in March 1964, and did not like his support for violence.

But Martin knew why African Americans were angry. There was still little equality between the races. African Americans lived in the worst neighborhoods, attended the worst schools, and had the worst-paid jobs—if they even had a job.

Rioters in the streets of Harlem, New York.

"I Have a DREAM"

In August 1963, thousands of people marched for civil rights in Washington, D.C. Martin gave one of the most famous speeches ever.

Martin Luther King's "I Have a Dream" speech is today seen as one of the most inspirational speeches in American history—but it almost never happened. Many speakers had been lined up to address the huge crowds on the National Mall after the March on Washington on August 28, 1963. Martin was the last speaker. Standing in front of the Lincoln Memorial, he started to read his prepared speech.

When Martin was partway through, a friend nearby called out, "Tell them about your dream, Martin." So Martin did.

Martin and other leaders in the March on Washington.

The view down the National Mall to the Washington Monument.

He changed his prepared script and instead told the crowd about a dream he had had the night before when he dreamed that one day black and white people could live together peacefully. He said he dreamed that "my four little children will one day live in a nation where they will not be judged by the color of their skin but by the content of their character." Martin underlined his points by repeating the phrase, "I have a dream today." His speech marked a turning point in the civil rights movement. It helped persuade the government that the Civil Rights Bill should contain **radical** ideas to improve African American life. When the bill became law in 1964, it met many of the demands of the civil rights movement.

The ASSASSINATION

By the end of 1965, Martin began to develop wider ambitions for change. He would not get a chance to fulfill them.

Martin thought his work in the South was over. It was time to do something about how most African Americans lived everywhere. He moved his family to a poor black neighborhood in Chicago, Illinois. He wanted to draw attention to how hard life was for most black Americans. He wanted to organize a new march on Washington that would unite poor Americans of any color. Martin wanted to campaign for better housing and peaceful lives.

Martin promotes one of his books.

QUICK FACTS

- Martin was shot dead in Memphis, Tennessee.
- James Earl Ray admitted to the murder–but years later he took back his confession!

U.S. soldiers and helicopters in Vietnam.

THE VIETNAM WAR

While Martin was campaigning for change at home, thousands of miles away America had become involved in the Vietnam War (1955–1975). As the 1960s went on, America **drafted** soldiers to fight the Communist North Vietnamese. Many of the soldiers were black. It soon became clear that North Vietnam was winning the war. Many Americans were angry that so many young men were dying in a war so far away. Protests against the war became more frequent. Martin publicly spoke out against the war.

Martin told President Johnson that his decision to continue the war was wrong. The two men had worked closely together to advance civil rights, but now they fell out. When Martin asked Johnson to support his Chicago campaign, Johnson refused.

MEMPHIS, TENNESSEE

In March 1968, city sanitation workers went on strike in Memphis, Tennessee. They were protesting their low pay and bad working conditions. Since most of the workers were African Americans, they asked Martin if he would lead a peaceful protest march. He agreed, and flew to the city on March 28, 1968.

Martin meets with President Lyndon B. Johnson.

Martin did not know that members of the Black Power movement would also be marching. The Black Power movement believed that African Americans could only improve their position through violence. Before long, the march turned violent. Police fired on the marchers, killing a young boy. Martin was devastated. He knew that TV images of young African Americans fighting would make people question his philosophy of nonviolence. Martin left Memphis. He promised to return a week later to lead a nonviolent rally.

APRIL 4, 1968

Martin kept his promise, even though he was nervous about violence at the rally. He returned to Memphis and checked into the second story of the Lorraine Motel on April 3. That evening he gave his speech "I've Been to the Mountaintop." He promised his audience that they would reach the "Promised Land." But he added, "I may not get there with you." Then Martin returned to the motel.

The Lorraine Motel.

Garment workers listen to Martin's funeral on the radio.

Martin spent April 4 quietly at the motel. He dressed for dinner and went onto his balcony at around 6:00 p.m. Friends were joking in the parking lot and Martin leaned over the balcony to talk to them. Suddenly a gun fired and he slumped to the ground. People rushed to help him but it was too late. Martin died as an ambulance took him to the hospital. He was 39 years old and had been part of the civil rights movement for 13 years. His body was returned to Atlanta, where 60,000 mourners attended his funeral.

James Earl Ray.

THE ASSASSIN

Riots broke out in a number of cities as news of Martin's murder spread. African Americans were angry that their hero had been killed. The FBI led the hunt for Martin's killer. They found that James Earl Ray, a small-time criminal and racist, had booked a room overlooking the Lorraine Motel that day.

After the shooting, Ray had fled the scene, but he had left behind a rifle with his fingerprints on it. He escaped to Britain, but was arrested and returned to America. He did not stand trial because he confessed to the murder. Before he died in 1998, Ray claimed he had not killed Martin and asked for a retrial. He met with the King family. They came to believe he had not killed Martin.

Coretta believed Ray did not kill Martin.

Martin and Coretta's tomb in Atlanta, Georgia.

However, most experts still believe that Ray fired the rifle that killed Martin. No one knows exactly why he did so, nor how he planned the murder.

CIVIL RIGHTS AFTER MARTIN

Martin did not live to see social **equality** in the United States, but since his death much has changed. In 2008, Americans elected Barack Obama as the first African American president. In the 1950s and 1960s that would have seemed impossible. However, many observers agree that racial inequality remains a huge problem facing twenty-first century America.

Timeline

1929
- January 15: Martin Luther King Jr. is born in Atlanta, Georgia.

1944
- Leaves school at age 15 to attend Morehouse College.

1948
- Ordained as a Baptist minister.
- Appointed as assistant pastor at Ebenezer Baptist Church, Atlanta.

1953
- Marries Coretta Scott.
- Moves to Montgomery, Alabama.
- Becomes pastor of the Dexter Avenue Church.

1955
- December 1: Rosa Parks arrested on bus.
- Montgomery Bus Boycott begins.

1956
- Martin is sent to jail for the first time. Montgomery Bus Boycott ends in victory.

1957
- Becomes leader of the Southern Christian Leadership Conference (SCLC).

1958
- Stabbed and nearly killed in New York City.

1960
- Supports lunch-counter sit-ins throughout the South.

1961
- The Freedom Rides begin.

1963
- April 12: Arrested in Birmingham, Alabama. Writes “Letter from Birmingham Jail.”
- August 28: March on Washington.
- Delivers “I Have a Dream” speech.
- November 22: President Kennedy assassinated.

1964	· Time magazine's "Man of the Year." · Wins Nobel Peace Prize. · July 2: Civil Rights Act passed.
1965	· Selma–Montgomery march. · August 6: Voting Rights Act passed.
1966	· Moves to Chicago, Illinois.
1967	· Speaks out against Vietnam War.
1968	· Delivers "I've Been to the Mountaintop" speech in Memphis, Tennessee. · April 4: Shot dead at the Lorraine Motel, Memphis. · 60,000 attend funeral in Atlanta, Georgia.
1969	· James Earl Ray confesses to murder.
1986	· Martin Luther King Day becomes an official holiday. Martin is only the third person to be so honored, after George Washington and Christopher Columbus.

KEY SPEECHES AND BOOKS

- *Stride Toward Freedom: The Montgomery Story* (1957)
- *The Measure of a Man* (1959)
- *Strength to Love* (1963)
- "Letter from Birmingham Jail," April 16, 1963
- "I Have a Dream," August 28, 1963
- *Why We Can't Wait* (1964)
- *Where Do We Go From Here: Chaos or Community?* (1967)
- Nobel Prize Acceptance Speech, December 10, 1964
- "Beyond Vietnam," April 4, 1967
- "I've Been to the Mountaintop," April 3, 1968

Glossary

assassination A murder committed for a political reason.

boycott To refuse to buy goods or services from a particular organization, country, or person.

civil rights The right of all citizens to equal political and social freedom and opportunity.

discrimination The unfair treatment of a group of people based on their race, religion, or other factors.

drafted Forced someone to serve in the military services.

equality A state where everyone has equal rights and freedoms.

frustration Feeling upset because you cannot change things.

Jim Crow laws State and local laws that enforced segregation of facilities in the South.

lobby To try to influence a politician on an issue.

monitor To keep a check on something over a period of time.

orator Someone skilled at giving speeches in public.

ordained Taken into holy orders as a priest or minister.

prejudice An instinctive opinion of something that is not based on knowledge or experience.

racist Believing that one race of people is superior to another.

radical Far-reaching and thorough.

revolution A violent attempt to bring down a government.

segregated Describes a group of people who are separated from the rest of society.

sermons Talks on religious subjects in a church service.

shrine A holy place associated with a particular god or person.

sit-in A protest in which people refuse to leave a place.

unconstitutional Illegal under the U.S. Constitution.

wiretaps Listening devices attached to phone lines to allow people to listen secretly to calls.

Further Resources

Books

Adamson, Heather. *The Civil Rights Movement: An Interactive History*. You Chose History. Mankato, MN: Capstone Press, 2009.

Aretha, David. *Martin Luther King Jr. and the March on Washington*. Civil Rights Movement. Greensboro, NC: Morgan Reynolds Publishing, 2014.

Bader, Bonnie. *Who Was Martin Luther King, Jr?* Who Was? New York: Grosset and Dunlap, 2007.

Gregory, Josh. *Martin Luther King, Jr*. True Books. New York: Children's Press, 2015.

Mis, Melody S. *Meet Coretta Scott King*. Civil Rights Leaders. New York: PowerKids Press, 2008.

Pinkney, Andrea Davis. *Sit-In: How Four Friends Stood Up by Sitting Down*. New York: Little, Brown Books for Young Readers, 2010.

Websites

BBC History
www.bbc.co.uk/timelines/z86tn39
A detailed timeline of Martin Luther King's life.

CNN
edition.cnn.com/EVENTS/1997/mlk/links.html
A timeline of the civil rights movement.

King Institute
kinginstitute.stanford.edu/king-kids
A children's site run by the King Institute at Stanford University.

History.com
www. history.com/topics/black-history/martin-luther-king-jr
A biography of Martin Luther King with videos and links.

Publisher's note to educators and parents: Our editors have carefully reviewed these websites to ensure that they are suitable for students. Many websites change frequently, however, and we cannot guarantee that a site's future contents will continue to meet our high standards of quality and educational value. Be advised that students should be closely supervised whenever they access the Internet.

Index

A

African Americans 4, 8, 9, 11, 12, 13, 14, 15, 18, 19, 30, 33
Alabama 11, 22, 26
assassination, Martin Luther King 41
Atlanta 6, 8, 10, 20, 41

B

Birmingham, AL 22, 23, 26
Black Power 40
bus boycott 12, 13, 18, 24

C

Chicago 36, 39
Civil Rights Act 30
Civil Rights Bill 28, 29, 35
civil rights movement 4, 14, 15, 16, 24, 25, 26
communism 24, 25
Connor, Eugene "Bull" 22, 23, 26
Crusade for Citizenship 19

D

Dallas, Texas 29
Dexter Avenue Church 11
Dylan, Bob 28

E F

Federal Bureau of Investigation 24, 25, 42
Freedom Riders 21

G H

Gandhi, Mahatma 16, 20
Georgia 6
Greensboro, NC 20
Harlem, New York 33
Hoover, J. Edgar 24, 25

I J

"I Have a Dream" speech 29, 34, 35
"I've Been to the Mountaintop" speech 40
India 20
Jim Crow laws 8, 14
Johnson, Lyndon B. 29, 30, 32, 39

K

Kennedy, John F. 23, 28, 29, 30
Kennedy, Robert 25
King, Coretta 10, 11, 20, 42
King, Martin Sr. 6, 8
King, Yolanda 11

L

"Letter from Birmingham Jail" 22
Lincoln, Abraham 14
Lorraine Motel 40, 42

M

Malcolm X 14, 19, 33
March for Jobs and Freedom 28
March on Washington 28, 34
Memphis, Tennessee 39, 40, 41
Montgomery 11, 12, 13, 16, 24, 32
Morehouse College 10

N

Nation of Islam 33
National Association for the Advancement of Colored People 11
Nobel Peace Prize 30, 31

O P R

Obama, Barack 43
Parks, Rosa 12
police 8
Ray, James Earl 42
rioting 33, 42

S

segregation 8, 9, 10, 13, 20, 21, 30
Selma, Alabama 31, 32
sit-ins 20, 21
Southern Christian Leadership Conference 18, 20, 25
Supreme Court 13, 14, 15

T V

Time magazine 30
Vietnam War 38, 39
voter registration 19, 30, 31
Voting Rights Act 15
Voting Rights Bill 32

W

Wallace, George 22, 32
Washington, D.C. 28, 34